ARNOLD SCHWARZENEGGER

A Real-Life Reader Biography

Susan Zannos

Mitchell Lane Publishers, Inc.
P.O. Box 196 • Hockessin, Delaware 19707

71288

Mitchell Lane
PUBLISHERS

Printing   4   5   6   7   8   9   10

Real-Life Reader Biographies

Paula Abdul	Christina Aguilera	Marc Anthony	Lance Armstrong
Drew Barrymore	Tony Blair	Brandy	Garth Brooks
Kobe Bryant	Sandra Bullock	Mariah Carey	Aaron Carter
Cesar Chavez	Roberto Clemente	Christopher Paul Curtis	Roald Dahl
Oscar De La Hoya	Trent Dimas	Celine Dion	Sheila E.
Gloria Estefan	Mary Joe Fernandez	Michael J. Fox	Andres Galarraga
Sarah Michelle Gellar	Jeff Gordon	Virginia Hamilton	Mia Hamm
Melissa Joan Hart	Salma Hayek	Jennifer Love Hewitt	Faith Hill
Hollywood Hogan	Katie Holmes	Enrique Iglesias	Allen Iverson
Janet Jackson	Derek Jeter	Steve Jobs	Alicia Keys
Michelle Kwan	Bruce Lee	Jennifer Lopez	Cheech Marin
Ricky Martin	Mark McGwire	Alyssa Milano	Mandy Moore
Chuck Norris	Tommy Nuñez	Rosie O'Donnell	Mary-Kate and Ashley Olsen
Rafael Palmeiro	Gary Paulsen	Colin Powell	Freddie Prinze, Jr.
Condoleezza Rice	Julia Roberts	Robert Rodriguez	J.K. Rowling
Keri Russell	Winona Ryder	Cristina Saralegui	Charles Schulz
Arnold Schwarzenegger	Selena	Maurice Sendak	Dr. Seuss
Shakira	Alicia Silverstone	Jessica Simpson	Sinbad
Jimmy Smits	Sammy Sosa	Britney Spears	Julia Stiles
Ben Stiller	Sheryl Swoopes	Shania Twain	Liv Tyler
Robin Williams	Vanessa Williams	Venus Williams	Tiger Woods

Library of Congress Cataloging-in-Publication Data
Zannos, Susan.
        Arnold Schwarzenegger/Susan Zannos.
            p. cm. — (A real-life reader biography)
        Includes index.
        Summary: A biography of the Austrian-born bodybuilder who has become a popular movie star.
        ISBN 1-883845-95-5 (lib. bdg.)
        1. Schwarzenegger, Arnold Juvenile literature. 2. Motion picture actors and actresses—United States Biography
Juvenile literature. [1. Schwarzenegger, Arnold. 2. Actors and actresses. 3. Bodybuilders.] I. Title. II. Series.
PN2287.S3368Z36 1999
791.43'028'092—dc21
    [B]
                                                                                                    99-19978
                                                                                                    CII

ABOUT THE AUTHOR: Susan Zannos has taught at all levels, from preschool to college, in Mexico, Greece, Italy, Russia, and Lithuania, as well as in the United States. She has published a mystery **Trust the Liar** (Walker and Co.) and **Human Types: Essence and the Enneagram** was published by Samuel Weiser in 1997. She has written several books for children, including **Paula Abdul** and **Cesar Chavez** (Mitchell Lane).
PHOTO CREDITS: cover: Weider Health & Fitness/Neveux/Shooting Star; pp. 4, 25 The Kobal Collection; pp. 6, 11, 13, 19 Michael Montfort/Shooting Star; p. 28 Corbis/Bettmann-UPI; p. 29 Corbis/Reuters; p. 30 Laura Cavanaugh/Globe Photos.
ACKNOWLEDGMENTS: The following story has been thoroughly researched, and to the best of our knowledge, represents a true story. Though we try to authorize every biography that we publish, for various reasons, this is not always possible. This story is not authorized nor endorsed by Arnold Schwarzenegger or any of his representatives.

Table of Contents

Chapter 1
Birth of a Champion

Arnold Schwarzenegger's life has been like a fairy tale. The story began in a small village in a small country that has mountains and castles and forests. When Arnold was a little boy, his family was poor, and he was often sick. But Arnold knew a secret magic that would help his dreams come true. The magic that Arnold used is simple: he worked very, very hard. With his magic, Arnold knew that one day all his dreams would come true.

Arnold was born on July 30, 1947, in the Austrian village of Thal. His father, Gustav Schwarzenegger, was the

This story begins in a country that has mountains and castles and forests.

police chief in Thal. Arnold's mother, Aurelia, married Gustav after the Second World War, in October 1945. Their first son, Meinhard, was born a year before Arnold, in July 1946.

Thal was a poor village. There were only three telephones and one television in the whole town. The Schwarzenegger home had no heat and no indoor bathroom. The boys' mother had to carry water to the house. In spite of this she kept everything very clean. Aurelia

Taken in 1958, this photograph shows Arnold when he was 11 years old.

Schwarzenegger worked hard to cook and clean, to sew and mend her family's clothes, and to care for Arnold when he was sick, which was often. There was no doctor in the village, so if a child was sick he had to be carried on his parents' shoulders to the town of Graz, which was five miles away.

Gustav was a strict father who believed in discipline and hard work for his sons. The two boys always woke early to do their chores before school. The boys were made to compete with each other, both in their studies and in sports such as boxing, skiing, and soccer. Because Arnold was a year younger, and because he was not as strong and healthy as Meinhard, he usually lost. Meinhard was his father's favorite, which made Arnold feel bad. He wanted to be a winner so his father would praise him, but this seldom happened.

As Arnold grew older, he became a successful athlete. He liked individual sports like swimming, boxing, and track

Arnold's father was strict and he believed in hard work for his sons.

and field, and he also became a good soccer player. However, even though Arnold played soccer for five years, he didn't like playing on a team.

His time on the soccer squad did lead to another sport that he became more interested in. When he was 15, his soccer coach decided it would be good for the team to lift weights to build their strength and develop their legs. Arnold still remembers his first visit to the gym. He had never seen anyone lifting weights before. He walked around looking at the huge muscles these powerful men had. "And there it was before me," Arnold says, "my life, the answer I'd been seeking."

The bodybuilders at the gym soon noticed that Arnold was working much harder than the other boys on the soccer team, and they started helping him. He went with them to the lake where they did exercises without weights—chin-ups on the tree branches, sit-ups, push-ups, leg raises—all designed to get their bodies ready for the gym.

When Arnold was 15, his soccer coach thought it would be good for the team to lift weights.

At the end of the summer Arnold began real weight training. "I loved the feel of cold iron and steel warming to my touch and the sounds and smells of the gym," he once said. For his first real workout, he rode his bicycle eight miles to the gym. He tried everything: barbells, dumbbells, and machines. The experienced weightlifters warned him that he was doing too much for the first time. He wouldn't listen. When he finally started home, he was so weak he couldn't ride his bike. He had to walk home, leaning on the bicycle.

The next morning Arnold was so sore he couldn't even lift his arms to comb his hair. His mother was worried about him. She couldn't understand why he wanted to do something that caused him so much pain. But Arnold didn't care what anyone said. Even though his parents and his school friends thought he was crazy, he began to spend all his free time in the gym.

Arnold tried everything: barbells, dumbbells, and machines.

Chapter 2
Growing Stronger

Arnold read all he could about body-building.

As Arnold became more involved in weight training, he read all that he could about bodybuilding. Whenever he could get his hands on bodybuilding magazines from America, he looked at the pictures of champions. He went to the movies and saw stars like Steve Reeves who had big muscles because they worked out. The star he liked best was Reg Park, whose pictures were in all the bodybuilding magazines. "That's what I wanted to be: big," Arnold admitted. "I wanted to be a big guy. . . I wanted every muscle to explode and be huge. I dreamed about being gigantic."

Arnold knew that dedication to his chosen sport would make it possible for him to become a big champion like Reg Park. While other bodybuilders in Thal worked out two or three times a week, Arnold worked out six days a week. Once he even broke into the gym when he arrived and it was locked up!

His father couldn't understand it. "What are you going to do with all those muscles after you get them?" he asked Arnold.

Aurelia and Gustav, Arnold's mother and father

"I want to be the best-built man in the world," Arnold said. "Then I want to go to America and be in movies."

"My God!" his father said to his mother. "I think we better go to the doctor with this one, he's sick in the head."

Gustav Schwarzenegger was right. Arnold didn't want to be normal. He wanted to be great, and he saw bodybuilding as the way to do it. When winter came and his father only allowed him to go to the gym three times a week, Arnold built his own weight room in his house to use on the other days. However, he preferred the gym because there he worked out with a partner. The two of them would push each other to work harder.

When Arnold was 18 years old, he enlisted in the army. While he was still in basic training, he received an invitation to compete in the junior division of the Mr. Europe contest in Germany.

The soldiers were not allowed to leave the base, so Arnold crawled over a wall and escaped. He had barely enough money to buy a train ticket. When he got to Germany, he had to borrow the things he needed for the contest.

This was the first competition that Arnold had ever been in. On the train, he had thought about all the pictures he had seen of Reg Parks in bodybuilding magazines. He memorized some of the poses that Parks used to show off his muscles, and planned to do them himself in the contest.

In 1965, when Arnold was 18 years old, he entered his first competition.

By the time he got there he was tired and confused, but when he stepped in front of the judges he somehow went through the poses he had memorized. Then the announcement came: Arnold Schwarzenegger had won! He was Mr. Europe Junior.

Being a champion did not initially lead to fame and fortune. Arnold had to borrow money to get back to his Austrian army base. He got caught crawling back over the wall, and they put him in jail for seven days. But he didn't care. He had his trophy. Arnold's dreams were coming true.

Chapter 3
Champion

After Arnold won the Mr. Europe Junior contest, things began to change in the way people acted. They no longer thought he was crazy. His parents were proud of him. His mother ran through the village showing his trophy to everyone. The officers in the army gave him time off from his regular duties so that he could continue training.

When Arnold got out of the army, a man who had been a judge in the contest invited Arnold to come and work at the gym he owned in Munich, Germany. Munich was much different from Arnold's hometown, Thal. It was

His mother ran through the village showing his trophy to everyone.

one of the biggest and busiest cities in central Europe, and there would be many new opportunities for the up-and-coming weightlifter.

During the day, Arnold taught customers at the Munich gym how to exercise properly. He also continued lifting weights, and began doing two workouts a day, in the morning and in the evening. Arnold had two goals: to win the Mr. Europe contest and compete in the Mr. Universe contest, held in London.

Months of hard training paid off when Arnold won the Mr. Europe contest and was invited to the Mr. Universe competition. The 19-year-old bodybuilder didn't know how he was going to get the money to go to London, but he knew he was going to go. Some of the bodybuilders in Munich raised money to help him. Finally he had enough for his ticket. It was the first time he had been on an airplane, and the first time he had been to a country where no one spoke German.

Months of hard training paid off when Arnold won the Mr. Europe contest and was invited to the Mr. Universe competition.

Because everyone was amazed at his size, he began to think he could win. Then he saw the top American bodybuilder. Arnold realized he still had a long way to go. He was big, but that wasn't enough. The American was not only big, but each one of his muscles was clearly defined. Arnold had thought he knew everything about bodybuilding. Now he realized there was still much to learn.

Not only was the American more fully developed than Arnold, he was also more confident. Arnold realized that having the attitude of a winner was important. He didn't win the Mr. Universe contest, but he was second. More important, he understood exactly what he needed to do to prepare for the next year.

When Arnold got back to Munich, his friends were wild with excitement. They had thought it would be great if Arnold finished fifth or sixth. When they heard he was second they had a huge party to celebrate. But the only

Arnold thought he knew everything about body—building. Now he knew he had a lot to learn.

thing Arnold could think of was getting to the gym to start working for next year's contest.

During that year many things happened. The owner of the gym where Arnold worked offered to sell him the business, and Arnold was able to raise the money. Also, he was invited to tour in England giving bodybuilding demonstrations. In January of 1967 he met his hero, Reg Park, and was able to tour with him for a week and get his advice about training. Most important of all, being with Reg Park made Arnold realize that he wanted to be a better person, not just a better body.

As he became more satisfied with his own progress in bodybuilding, Arnold admitted that in other ways he wasn't very good. He had been rude to people and acted like a tough guy trying to prove he was a winner. Now he knew that he could win contests. He didn't have to prove anything. He started to work at being better in other ways, too.

Arnold went to the Mr. Universe contest in 1967 with the attitude that he was a winner, and he was. When he heard the judge announce: "Mr. Universe of 1967 . . . Arnold Schwarzenegger!" he knew for sure that his magic spell worked.

Arnold won many bodybuilding competitions, including Mr. Universe, Mr. Olympia, and Mr. World.

Chapter 4
Coming to America

Arnold Schwarzenegger won the Mr. Universe title again in 1968. After his second win, Joe Weider, who published magazines about bodybuilding, invited Arnold to come to the United States. As a two-time Mr. Universe, Arnold thought he would win his first contest easily. It was a big shock when he came in second. He realized that being big wasn't enough. To beat the Americans he would have to develop all parts of his body equally, not just his arms and chest.

Arnold didn't waste time feeling bad about not winning. By the next day

Joe Weider invited Arnold to come to the United States.

he said, "I'm going to show them who is really the best." He planned to use the Americans' food, vitamins, and training methods to beat them. He made an arrangement with Mr. Weider. He would spend a year training in America in exchange for helping to sell Weider's bodybuilding products.

Arnold moved to California where Mr. Weider's business was located. He knew he had found his home. He loved everything about California—Gold's Gym, where the bodybuilders worked out, the fresh air, and the ocean beaches. Arnold was only 21 years old, but he knew that he could get whatever he set his mind to through hard work and his belief in himself.

Arnold won contest after contest. In addition to three more Mr. Universe titles, Arnold won seven Mr. Olympia titles and the Mr. World title once. His 13 major international victories are more than anyone else has ever won. Arnold had achieved his dream of having the most perfect body in the world.

Arnold moved to California where Mr. Weider's business was located.

Arnold invested all of the money he made from contests and exhibitions. He started buying real estate. At first he bought apartment buildings, then an office building. He looked for good investments all over the country. He bought a whole city block in Denver, and an office building in Nevada. He bought restaurants, too. By 1975 he had enough money to retire—if he wanted to.

But Arnold Schwarzenegger wasn't ready to retire yet. He had accomplished one dream, now he had another: to be a movie star. However, even though he had been in a couple of movies, people in Hollywood didn't think he could ever be a star. For one thing, they thought his name was too long and too hard to pronounce. They wanted him to change his name. They also thought his German accent would keep him from being a good actor. Arnold remembers agents who said, "Forget it. You've got a weird-looking body and a weird-sounding name and a weird-sounding accent. You could never be a movie star." But Arnold knew better.

In 1976, Arnold played a European bodybuilder in a movie called *Stay Hungry*. The next year, his quest for another Mr. Olympia title was the subject of a successful documentary about bodybuilding called *Pumping Iron*. But even though he had studied acting, and had won a Golden Globe award as "the most promising newcomer," it wasn't until 1981 that Arnold starred in a hit film, *Conan the Barbarian*.

The director of *Conan* was afraid that Arnold's accent would ruin the movie, so Arnold worked very hard with a voice teacher so that he could be understood. However, when the film was finished, everyone realized that Arnold's accent was perfect for the part of a barbarian hero. *Conan the Barbarian* was very popular. It made the world realize that Arnold Schwarzenegger was not just a big man, but that he would be a big movie star, too.

Arnold wanted to be a movie star. Some agents told him to forget it. He could never be in movies.

For the next few years, all the films that Arnold made were similar to *Conan the Barbarian*. They were violent action films. His next movie was the 1984 hit *The Terminator*, in which he played an evil robot. Then he made two Conan sequels, *Conan the Destroyer* and *Red Sonja*. Action hits like *Commando* (1985), *The Running Man* (1987), and *Predator* (1987) made him the most famous action hero.

But Arnold didn't stop there. As always, after he achieved a goal he immediately began on another. Arnold wanted to prove that he could play comedy parts as well as hero parts. In 1988 he made a movie with a short, pudgy comic actor named Danny DeVito called *Twins*. Audiences laughed at the idea that big strong Arnold and tiny Danny were twin brothers separated at birth, and the movie was a hit. In 1990, Arnold starred in two more hit movies, the action film *Total Recall* and the comedy *Kindergarten Cop*, in which he plays a tough police officer who must take a job as a kindergarten teacher while tracking down a suspect.

When *Terminator 2: Judgement Day* was released in 1992, the picture earned over $400 million dollars. Arnold combined action and comedy in his 1994 hit *True Lies*, and made that movie one of the year's biggest box-office hits. There was no doubt in Hollywood or anywhere else that Arnold Schwarzenegger was one of the biggest movie stars ever.

In Terminator 2: Judgment Day, *Arnold starred as a cyborg sent to protect a young boy.*

Chapter 5
Arnold and Maria

Arnold met Maria Schriver at a tennis tournament in August 1977.

Arnold Schwarzenegger met Maria Shriver at a tennis tournament in August 1977. Maria lived like a princess. She had grown up in a family of wealth and privilege. Her father, Sargent Shriver, had been a candidate for vice president in 1972, and her mother, Eunice Kennedy Shriver, was the sister of former president John F. Kennedy, presidential candidate Bobby Kennedy, and U.S. Senator Edward Kennedy.

For Maria it was love at first sight. Arnold liked Maria very much, and the more he saw of her, the more he liked her. He also enjoyed talking to the well-educated people in Maria's family. He could speak in his native German language with Maria's father and with her grandmother, Rose Kennedy.

All of Maria's family were members of the Democratic political party. Arnold was a Republican, but Maria didn't care. She told her uncle, Senator Ted Kennedy, "Don't look at him as a Republican, look at him as the man I love. And if that doesn't work, look at him as someone who can squash you."

Maria had her own career. She was a television newscaster. Maria and Arnold had to travel back and forth across the country to see each other when she was working on the East Coast and he was making movies on the West Coast. Finally, in 1985, Arnold took Maria on a trip to Austria. He took her out in a boat on the lake near the village of Thal where he grew up. He gave her a ring and asked her to marry him. Maria said, "Yes!" They were married in a big wedding on April 26, 1986.

Though she was from a very famous family, Maria had her own career. She was a television news—caster.

Arnold and Maria were married in Hyannisport, MA at St. Francis Xavier Church.

One of the things that Arnold liked best about Maria and her family was the way they tried to help other people. In the 1960s, Maria's mother had started the Special Olympics for people who were physically or mentally impaired. Arnold realized that this was something he could help with. He became the national weight-lifting coach for the Special Olympics.

Arnold has always like to helped others. When his older brother Meinhard died in an auto accident, he helped his

nephew, Patrick. When he started making money in business and in the movies, Arnold helped the children of his friends to get an education in the United States. He gave millions of dollars to the Simon Wiesenthal Center for Peace and Racial Tolerance. He has donated time, effort, and over a million dollars to the Hollenbeck Youth Center in East Los Angeles, and he became executive director of the Inner City Games, an athletic event involving 100,000 kids from 21 Los Angeles low income housing projects.

Arnold dances with Maria's mother, Eunice Shriver.

In 1988 President George Bush appointed Arnold Schwarzen– egger to be Chairman of the President's Council on Physical Fit– ness and

Sports. Arnold has been active in supporting physical fitness. He has written several books and made videos telling how children can get in shape.

Arnold and Maria have four children. Their daughter Katherine was born on December 13th, 1989. A second daughter, Christina Aurelia, was born in July, 1991. Their son Patrick was born in November 1993 and a second son, Christopher, in October 1997.

Arnold and Maria with daughters Katherine and Christina, 1995.

Arnold is continuing to work on all of his goals. He keeps physically fit, makes movies, devotes time to his family, helps inner city kids, and was elected governor of California in 2003. If his life seems like a happily-ever-after fairy tale, it is because he uses his magic spell of hard work and belief in his ability to achieve his goals.

Chronology

1947 Born on July 30 in the village of Thal, Austria, to Aurelia and Gustav Schwarzenegger

1965 Began serving in Austrian Army; won Junior Mr. Europe contest on October 30

1966 Won Mr. Germany contest

1967 Won first Mr. Universe contest

1968 Won second Mr. Universe competition; toured the United States with Joe Weider

1975 Made documentary film, *Pumping Iron*

1976 Won Golden Globe award as "most promising newcomer" for film *Stay Hungry*

1977 *Pumping Iron* released; autobiography, *Arnold: The Education of a Body Builder*, published; meets Maria Shriver

1980 Received a bachelors degree in economics from the University of Wisconsin

1981 Made first big film, *Conan the Barbarian*

1983 Became a United States citizen

1986 Married Maria Shriver on April 26

1988 Appointed Chairman of President's Council on Physical Fitness; makes *Twins* with Danny DeVito

1989 Daughter Katherine born

1991 Daughter Christina born

1992 Major hit *Terminator 2: Judgement Day* released

1993 Son Patrick born; named "International Star of the Decade by the National Association of Theater Owners.

1994 Hit movies *True Lies* and *Junior* are released

1996 Makes *Eraser* with Vanessa Williams; *Jingle All the Way* becomes a Christmas hit

1997 Plays "Mr. Freeze" in *Batman and Robin*; has heart surgery to replace aortic valve; son Christopher born.

1999 Makes film *End of Days* based on millenium

2002 Chapman University in Orange, California awards him honorary doctorate degree in humane letters for his work on behalf of young people in athletics and education.

2003 Elected Governor of California

Filmography

Hercules in New York (1970) (as Arnold Strong)
The Long Goodbye (1973) (uncredited)
Stay Hungry (1976)
Pumping Iron (1977)
The Villain (1979)
Scavenger Hunt (1979)
The Jayne Mansfield Story (1980; TV movie)
Conan the Barbarian (1981)
The Terminator (1984)
Conan the Destroyer (1984)
Red Sonja (1985)
Commando (1985)
Raw Deal (1986)

The Running Man (1987)
Predator (1987)
Twins (1988)
Red Heat (1988)
Total Recall (1990)
Kindergarten Cop (1990)
Terminator 2: Judgment Day (1991)
The Last Action Hero (1993)
True Lies (1994)
Junior (1994)
Eraser (1996)
Jingle All the Way (1996)
Batman and Robin (1997)
End of Days (1999)

Index